STECK-VAUGHN

PORTRAIT OF AMERICA

Maine

Steck-Vaughn Company
  Executive Editor   Diane Sharpe
  Senior Editor   Martin S. Saiewitz
  Design Manager   Pamela Heaney
  Photo Editor   Margie Foster
  Electronic Cover Graphics Alan Klemp

Proof Positive/Farrowlyne Associates, Inc.
Program Editorial, Revision Development, Design, and Production

Consultant: John A. Johnson, Director of Tourism Information, Maine Office of Tourism

Published by Raintree Steck-Vaughn Publishers, an imprint of Steck-Vaughn Company.

A Turner Educational Services, Inc. book. Based on the Portrait of America television series by R. E. (Ted) Turner.

Cover Photo: Fishing village © by Michael Reagan.

Library of Congress Cataloging-in-Publication Data

Thompson, Kathleen.
    Maine / Kathleen Thompson.
      p.   cm. — (Portrait of America)
    "Based on the Portrait of America television series"—T.p. verso.
    "A Turner book."
    Includes index.
    ISBN 0-8114-7339-2 (library binding).—ISBN 0-8114-7444-5 (softcover)
    1. Maine—Juvenile literature. I. Title. II. Series: Thompson,
Kathleen. Portrait of America.
F19.3.T46   1996
974.1—dc20   95-26117
                                              CIP
                                              AC

Printed and Bound in the United States of America

3 4 5 6 7 8 9 10 WZ 03 02 01 00 99

Acknowledgments
The publishers wish to thank the following for permission to reproduce photographs:
P. 7 © Tom Mackie/Tony Stone Images; p. 8 © Larry Lefever/Grant Heilman Photography; p. 10 (top) Maine Department of Inland Fisheries & Wildlife, (left) Maine State Museum; p. 11 Maine Historical Society; p. 12 Bangor Historical Society; p. 13 Maine Historical Society; p. 15 (top) The Granger Collection, (bottom) Maine Historical Society; p. 16 Maine Historical Society; pp. 17, 18 Maine Maritime Museum; p. 19 Bath Iron Works Corporation; p. 20 © Michael Reagan; p. 21 Maine Office of Tourism; p. 22 © Scott Davis/Margaret Chase Smith Library; p. 23 AP/Wide World; pp. 24, 25 Margaret Chase Smith Library; p. 26 Acadian Cultural Exchange; p. 27 © Beurmond J. Banville; p. 28 © Larry Lefever/Grant Heilman Photography; p. 30 (top) Maine Department of Agriculture, (bottom) Maine Office of Tourism; p. 31 (top) Maine Blueberry Commission, (bottom) VIA Portland; p. 32 (top) Maine Department of Agriculture, (bottom) L. L. Bean; p. 33 (top) Acadia National Park, National Park Service, (bottom) National Christmas Tree Association, Inc.; p. 35 (both) Maine Maritime Museum; p. 36 Wadsworth Antheneum, Hartford; p. 38 (top) Acadia National Park, National Park Service, (left) Maine Office of Tourism; p. 39 (both) Maine Historical Society; p. 40 Lark Society; p. 41 © Tom McPherson/Lark Society; p. 42 Maine Office of Tourism; p. 44 L. L. Bean; p. 46 One Mile Up; p. 47 (left) One Mile Up, (center, right) © Photo Researchers.

STECK-VAUGHN

PORTRAIT OF AMERICA

Maine

Kathleen Thompson

A Turner Book

RSVP

RAINTREE
STECK-VAUGHN
PUBLISHERS

The Steck-Vaughn Company

Austin, Texas

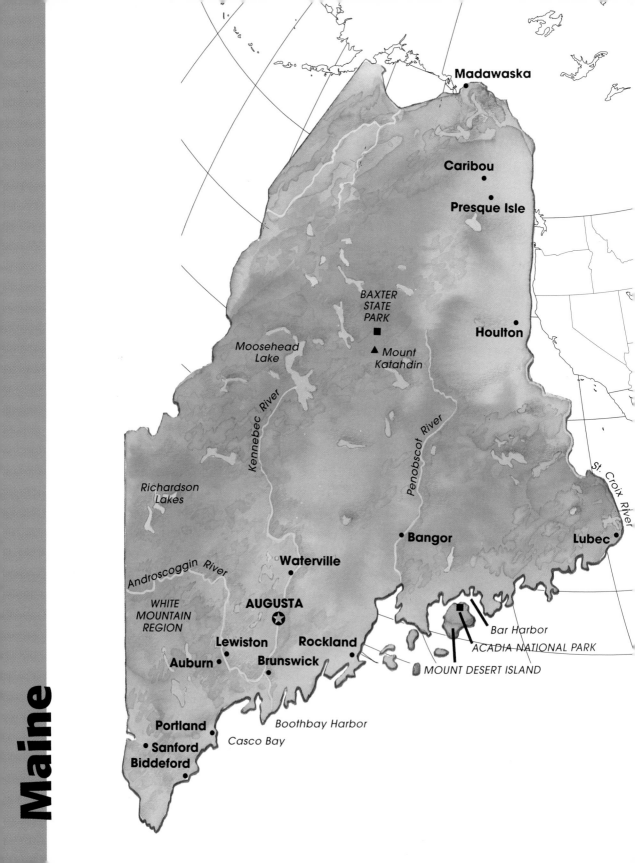

Madawaska

Caribou
●

Presque Isle
●

BAXTER
STATE
PARK
■

Houlton
●

▲ Mount
Katahdin

Moosehead
Lake

Kennebec River

Penobscot River

Richardson
Lakes

St. Croix River

● **Bangor**

Lubec ●

Androscoggin River

● **Waterville**

WHITE
MOUNTAIN
REGION

AUGUSTA
☆

Lewiston
●

Rockland
●

Bar Harbor

ACADIA NATIONAL PARK

Auburn ●

Brunswick

MOUNT DESERT ISLAND

Boothbay Harbor

Portland
●

Casco Bay

● **Sanford**

Biddeford
●

Maine

Contents

Introduction

Maine inspires an appreciation for beauty and the riches of nature. Thousands of small islands, coves, and harbors showcase the state's coastline. Gentle plateaus and fertile valleys in Maine's central and northern areas display a beauty apart from the sea. Thousands of lakes and streams are fed by natural springs and melted mountain snows. These lakes are all the more charming for their names: Mattawamkeag, Chiputneticook, Cobbosseecontea, Androscoggin, Tunk, Toddy, and Pushaw. The White Mountains and all of Maine's highlands are ornamented with balsam, beech, birch, pine, spruce, and oak. New England's largest state is a living catalog of nature's gifts.

Head Light stands as a sentry on the rocky coast of Portland. One of the oldest lighthouses in the United States, it was commissioned by President George Washington in 1791.

Maine

Acadia National Park, lobsters, shipbuilding

Maine: Leading the Nation

The first Europeans to reach the coast of present-day Maine were probably Vikings who arrived from Scandinavia. In A.D. 1000 the Vikings had established a colony northeast of the Maine region in what is now Newfoundland. They called the colony Vinland. All that's left of their presence in present-day Maine are some bronze weapons.

Two groups of Native Americans called the Abenaki were living in the Maine region when the Vikings arrived. The Passamaquoddy lived in the coastal area that today marks the boundary between Nova Scotia and Maine. The Penobscot lived along Penobscot Bay and in the Penobscot River valley. Both Abenaki groups fished and hunted, had small farms, and gathered berries and other vegetation.

Other Europeans began to explore the east coast of North America in the late fifteenth century. The Europeans visited but did not stay in the Maine region. Historians think the first explorer was probably a sea captain named John Cabot. Cabot's records aren't

Historic landmarks, such as Somesville Bridge, provide a reminder of the events that have shaped Maine's past.

Native Americans hunted moose for hundreds of years before the first European settlers arrived in Maine.

In 1968 this Norse penny was found on the Maine coast. Some experts believe it is evidence that Vikings landed in Maine in about the year 1000.

clear, but he may have explored the northern Atlantic Coast for England in about 1498. Giovanni da Verrazano explored the region in 1524 for France. In 1525 a Spanish captain named Estéban Gomez explored the coast. Gomez named three of the bays in the Maine region: Casco Bay, Saco Bay, and the Bay of Fundy.

In 1598, one hundred years after John Cabot's journey, Sir Humphrey Gilbert sent a ship to claim the Maine region for England. In 1603 Gilbert sent another ship from Massachusetts Colony to explore the entire coast of present-day Maine.

The English weren't the only ones interested in the region. At the same time, the French were exploring the area that is now eastern Canada. King Henry IV of France had given land north of present-day Maine to Sir Pierre du Gast, Sieur de Monts. This land included today's Nova Scotia, part of New Brunswick, and the northern region of today's Maine. In 1604 du Gast founded a colony on Dochet's Island in the St. Croix River, near today's Calais. This was the very first European colony north of Florida. After a harsh winter, the colonists moved to a nearby island called Port Royal. French explorer Samuel de Champlain used du Gast's colony as a base camp while he mapped the coastline of the Maine region. Champlain's maps were the most accurate French maps of the area.

In the meantime Sir Humphrey Gilbert's ship sailed to England with the English maps of the region. Sir Ferdinando Gorges studied the maps and decided to colonize the region. He and his partner, Sir John Popham, paid a group of colonists to establish a settlement in the Maine region. In 1607 the settlers founded the Popham Colony on the Kennebec River. The settlement didn't last, however. The winter was much more severe than the colonists had anticipated. In addition, they were repeatedly attacked by the Abenaki, who did not want trespassers. The colonists returned to England the following year.

French interest in the Maine region continued. In 1613 the French Roman Catholic Church established a mission on Mount Desert Island at the mouth of Penobscot Bay. The French missionaries established

Samuel de Champlain and his crew spent one year on Dochet's Island, where disease killed almost half of his party.

Madockawando was the chief of the Abnaki from 1669 to 1698.

favorable relations with the Native Americans there. The English didn't want any French settlements in the Maine region, however. In the first of many battles, the English drove out the French and burned the mission to the ground.

In 1622 the English Council for New England gave Gorges and John Mason all of the land between the Kennebec and Merrimack rivers. This area included much of today's Maine and New Hampshire. In 1629 the land was divided in half, and Gorges received the northern section.

That same year the Pilgrims of Massachusetts Colony established successful fur-trading posts at today's Castine on Penobscot Bay and at Machias, northeast of Castine. Castine and Machias were on land claimed by the French, however. So the French destroyed Machias and took over Castine, which later became a French stronghold.

Meanwhile Gorges continued to give financial support to colonies in the Maine region. In 1641 he established Gorgeana, now called York. It was the first chartered English colony in the Maine region. Gorges also supported other settlements. In 1652 the Massachusetts Colony took over the government of what was then called the province of Maine.

In 1667 England and France agreed on the Penobscot River as the boundary between their colonies. The English began to establish settlements along the coast. The French were interested in trade with the Native Americans, not settlements. They sent missionaries to convert the Abenaki to Christianity. The most famous missionary was Father Sebastian Rale, who created a dictionary of the Abenaki language and translated church prayers into Abenaki.

Good relations between the French and the English didn't last. Beginning about 1675 there were some conflicts between the two countries. Each group cooperated with nearby Native Americans and then persuaded the Native Americans to raid the other's settlements. Finally, France and Great Britain sent troops to fight each other for possession of North American land. This conflict, known as the French and Indian War, lasted until 1763. The war ended with the British and French signing the Treaty of Paris. This treaty gave most of North America east of the Mississippi River to the British.

Over the next 15 years, forty new settlements were started along the rivers and coastline of the province of Maine. These towns became centers for shipbuilding and trade. Merchants from the province established trade with the West Indies. Merchant ships traded fish, furs, lumber, and the mineral lime. In return, the province received sugar, molasses, rum, tobacco, and spices.

In order to pay for the expenses of fighting the French and Indian War, Great Britain imposed a tax on tea and other goods coming into the colonies. The colonists did not think these taxes were fair. They did

This hemp purse was woven in about 1800 by Mollyocket, an Anasagunticook. She was the most highly rated weaver of her era.

13

not like being made to pay without having any voice in government policy. In 1774 the citizens of York rebelled. To protest the tax on tea, they burned loads of British tea. In 1775 the province of Maine became involved in the first naval battle of the Revolutionary War. Citizens of Machias attacked and captured the British warship *Margaretta*. Shortly after, British ships attacked present-day Portland and burned it to the ground. Throughout the war the British took control of many of the province's coastal cities. By doing so the British hoped that they could put a halt to the building of ships that could threaten their navy. Colonists also had to fight Native American groups who raided towns in the province. Many Native American groups throughout the colonies fought as British allies.

The Revolutionary War ended in 1783 with the Treaty of Paris. The treaty set the eastern boundary of Maine at the St. Croix River. Without further supplies from the British, the Native Americans were weakened. Maine set up a plan to force Native Americans to live on reservations in the area. The peace was an invitation for more settlers to arrive from European countries. Banks and public libraries were established in many towns. The first cotton and woolen mills in America were built in Brunswick. Maine's shipping industry spread around the globe, and trade with China began.

In 1793 France and Great Britain went to war. Both countries began attacking American ships and stealing their cargoes. British ships even kidnapped

American sailors faced the danger of being kidnapped and forced into labor on British Navy ships. Some estimates of the number of sailors kidnapped reached as high as nine thousand.

American sailors and forced them to work in the British Navy. Finally, in 1812 the United States declared war on Great Britain. In Maine the British took over coastal cities as far south as Penobscot Bay. Once again Great Britain was trying to control the Maine shipbuilding industry. American merchant sailors and navy personnel responded by capturing British ships wherever they found them. In the first seven months of the war, Americans captured more than 1,300 British ships! Nevertheless the British succeeded in blockading movement in and out of ports along the coast of Maine. The War of 1812 came to an end in 1815 with the signing of the Treaty of Ghent.

In the 1800s Maine clipper ships sailed as far away as China. These ships got their name because they could sail at great speed, "clipping off" the miles.

In 1820 the province of Maine had a population large enough to apply for statehood. At that time the United States was admitting states on the basis of whether or not the state accepted slavery. Many northern states did not agree with the policy of enslavement. Southern states, however, insisted they needed slaves to plant and harvest cotton, their main crop. When Maine was admitted as a state, the country had an equal number of "free states" and "slave states." So, in what was called the Missouri Compromise, Maine was admitted as a free state to balance the admission of Missouri, a slave state. Maine became the twenty-third state on March 15, 1820.

In 1834 the temperance movement began in Maine. People who supported this movement felt that drinking alcohol caused many social problems. The movement gained so many supporters that in 1851 Maine passed a temperance law. This law made it illegal to manufacture or sell alcoholic beverages in the state.

The issue of slavery was slowly tearing the country apart. Abraham Lincoln was elected President of the United States in 1860. His Vice President, Hannibal Hamlin, was from Maine. The southern states disagreed with Lincoln's views on slavery and the amount of control the federal government had over the states. Eleven states, all of them from the South, withdrew from the Union. These states set up their own nation, which they called the Confederate States of America. Shortly after, the Union North and the Confederate South were engaged in the Civil War. Maine sent more than 72,000 men to fight for the

Colonel Joshua Chamberlain was the commander of the 20th Maine Regiment. During the Civil War, the regiment protected Washington, D.C., from being destroyed. For his brave leadership, Colonel Chamberlain was awarded the Congressional Medal of Honor.

Union. Maine was far from the actual battles of the war, which ended in 1865 with a Union victory.

A number of industries in Maine became successful in the period following the war, including the tourist trade. Tourism began around 1870, when people from areas south of Maine began to visit Bar Harbor. They came to its quiet bay in trains and steamships that traveled along the coast. The shipbuilding industry in Maine declined after the war because ships made of iron and steel became more popular than those made of wood. At that time Maine didn't have the capability to make iron and steel for ships. In 1880 the Bath Iron Works opened, and Maine shipbuilders began making steel ships. Other industries took a foothold as well. Cloth and leather industries became

In the nineteenth century, shipbuilding was a major industry at Bath.

Building a ship in the nineteenth century was done by hand, not by machine.

strong in the state. Manufacturers took advantage of Maine's abundant forests by opening paper mills. These companies cut down trees and delivered them to a sawmill. There the trees were ground into pulp, which was used to make paper. Lumber mills also flourished, as did farming. During the 1890s and early 1900s, small farms gave way to larger ones that specialized in growing potatoes or raising cattle and poultry.

World War I began in Europe in 1914, and the United States joined the fight in 1917. The war increased demand for Maine's ships. When the war ended in 1918, Maine's businesses slowed down. Many people who were hired to work during the war lost their jobs. Unemployment became even more serious during the Great Depression in the 1930s. The country's economy was in ruins. Banks and industries across the country closed.

The economy improved when the United States entered World War II in 1941. The federal government again asked manufacturers to supply war materials. Many people went back to work in the shipyards in Bath and in Portland, producing cargo vessels, destroyers, and submarines. Maine's mills and factories produced uniforms and shoes for the military. Casco Bay was the base for the United States Navy's North Atlantic fleet. When the war ended in 1945, shipbuilding continued to thrive. Lumber companies also experienced a boom. Returning soldiers were eager to settle down and begin families. Maine's lumber was needed to build homes in expanding suburbs across the nation.

Maine experienced great economic growth in the 1950s. Paper companies and food-processing companies grew by leaps and bounds. Improved roads helped the tourist industry, which developed ski facilities to draw winter visitors. Two Air Force bases were also established in the state. However, most of Maine's textile and leather companies moved to southern states, where labor costs were lower. In 1955, to draw new businesses to the state, Maine set up the Department of Economic Development.

In the 1960s Maine confronted threats to its environment. The state passed laws to clean up the rivers polluted by the lumber and paper industries. In 1976 Maine citizens voted to turn forty thousand acres of land on Bigelow Mountain in Somerset County into a wilderness preserve.

In 1980 the Passamaquoddy and the Penobscot sued the United States government. They wanted payment

The Bath Iron Works is one of the largest shipbuilding companies in the United States.

Maine citizens are dedicated to keeping their environment pollution-free.

for 12 million acres of land stolen from them in colonial times through false and illegal treaties. The groups were paid $81.5 million. Maine itself sought legal action against the federal government in 1988, when nine states sued the Environmental Protection Agency to control air pollution coming from the Midwest. Maine and other states argued that air pollution from the Midwest caused acid rain to fall on eastern states. Air pollution in the Midwest, which is caused by automobiles and industries, blows naturally toward the East Coast. When the pollution combines with the water vapor in clouds, it produces an acidic substance. By the time the clouds produce rain, they are over states such as Maine. Scientists have proven that acid rain has a very harmful effect on forests and lakes, both of which are a major part of Maine's economy.

Air pollution and acid rain continue to be problems in the 1990s. The Environmental Protection

Agency instituted strict controls on automobiles and on industries to clean up Maine's air. People in Maine are fighting those rules because they believe that the source of the state's air pollution is the Midwest, not industries in Maine.

Maine continues to build on its traditional strengths in shipbuilding and paper manufacturing. Also, the state's population is growing by about ten percent every ten years. Many newcomers settle in towns along the coast. Some people from Maine want to control housing development so the towns aren't overwhelmed by the number of newcomers. The state also continues to work on drawing new businesses to the state. Over the centuries Maine's citizens have been hardworking and practical people. With a tradition like that, Maine enters the new century with the promise of even more success.

Maine's population is growing, especially along the state's coast.

The First Woman of Politics

During a life that lasted almost the entire twentieth century, Margaret Chase Smith saw many changes. She saw horse-drawn buggies give way to jet airplanes. She saw the introduction of talking movies, television, and computers. Margaret Chase Smith helped make some changes, too. In her time, she was unique. She was the first woman to serve as a member of both the United States House of Representatives and the Senate.

Margaret Chase was born in Skowhegan, Maine, in 1897. As a child, she did not expect to work in government. In fact, her desire was to be an athletic coach. She did expect to work, however, and work hard. Margaret was the oldest of four children. Her father worked as a barber. Her mother was often employed as a clerk in the barber shop. With younger children in the family, Margaret hated to ask her parents for money. As soon as she was old enough, she went to work in the shop, too.

After high school, Margaret was employed as an elementary school teacher and as a reporter. She also became active in Republican politics. After marrying Clyde H. Smith in 1930, Margaret continued to serve in politics. She became a member of Maine's Republican Committee. Clyde Smith was a well-known figure in politics. When he made up his mind to fill a

This photo shows Margaret Chase Smith at age six. Even as a child, Smith proved she was someone who knew her own mind.

Senator Smith talks with French Premier Mendes France at the Senate. On the left is Senator Alexander Wiley, chairman of the Senate Foreign Relations Committee.

vacancy in the United States House of Representatives, Margaret Chase Smith was at the heart of his campaign. Clyde Smith won the Congressional seat in 1936, and he asked Margaret to work as his secretary.

In 1940 Clyde Smith had a heart attack. His doctors told him he was too weak to run for office again. Clyde immediately sent a letter to Maine newspapers and to Maine's Republican Committee. He urged them to choose Margaret to replace him in the House. He planned to work with her as she

had worked with him. Clyde Smith died before the election. Even while grieving for her husband, Margaret managed to campaign and win.

In Congress, Margaret Chase Smith was not afraid to say what she thought. She spoke up even when it made her unpopular. In her eight years in the House, Smith served on the Armed Forces and Naval Affairs committees. During World War II, she found out that the nurses caring for wounded servicemen did not receive all the benefits the men did. She

Margaret Chase Smith meets with other members of the Senate Armed Services Committee. Smith helped bring about passage of the 1948 Women's Armed Services Integration Act.

worked to give women in the military equal pay, rank, and benefits.

Margaret Chase Smith ran for the United States Senate in 1948 and won by a wide margin. At that time many Americans were beginning to fear the Soviet Union, which had a Communist government. Some people were afraid the Communists could gain influence over the United States government. One senator in particular, Senator Joseph McCarthy of Wisconsin, began accusing certain Americans of being Communists. Often he had no evidence to support his claims. His

Senate committee became very powerful. Most members of Congress were too afraid of Senator McCarthy to speak out against him. Margaret Chase Smith and six other senators felt that what he was doing was wrong, however. Smith said that it was wrong for McCarthy to accuse Americans without any evidence. By 1954 the majority of the Senate had come to agree with that view, and Senator McCarthy's accusations were stopped.

Margaret Chase Smith was elected to three more terms in the Senate. She was a member of important committees such as Government Operations, Armed Services, and Rules. She showed by example that women could make intelligent decisions on issues usually decided by men.

In 1964 a group of Republican women asked Margaret to run for President of the United States. She campaigned hard, even though her chances were slim. Many people at that time could not even imagine a woman as President. At the Republican National Convention in July 1964, Senator George Aiken nominated her for the presidency. This was the first time a woman had been nominated for United States President by a major party. Barry Goldwater was the eventual Republican choice, however.

In 1972 Margaret lost her first Senate election in 24 years. Her political career had come to an end after 33 years of public service. In retirement she gave speeches to college students and established a library. She also met with younger students. She told them what serving in government is like.

Margaret Chase Smith did much to advance the status of women in society and in politics. A few years before she died in 1995, President George Bush awarded her the Presidential Medal of Freedom. The medal is the nation's highest civilian honor, a fitting tribute to a woman who did so much for her country.

Margaret Chase Smith campaigns in New Hampshire in 1964, the year she announced her bid for the presidency. Smith finished second in the Republican primary in Maine.

Keeping Acadia in Madawaska

From about 1620 until 1763, the northern part of Maine, along with Nova Scotia and New Brunswick in Canada, was claimed by both France and Great Britain. The French called this land Acadia. When the British finally won control of the region, they told French settlers that they had to pledge loyalty to Great Britain. Many Acadians refused, so the British forced them to leave.

Some went west to Quebec. Others formed a French colony in present-day Louisiana, which later became part of the Cajun culture. Another group set up homes in the wilderness along the St. John River, which forms the border between Canada and Maine. Today, descendants of these French settlers in Maine are still called Acadians. Some Acadian families along the St. John River can trace their ancestry back 12 generations, as long ago as 1632! Many Acadians still speak French. Children speak French at home and use both French and English in school. The

When Acadians arrived at the St. John River valley, they placed a cross on the shore to give thanks for their safe passage. The cross shown here was erected in honor of that first Acadian cross.

Acadians follow the customs of their ancestors in their music, religion, and food preparation.

Madawaska is an Acadian town along the St. John River. In 1978 the town declared June 28th as Acadian Day in the state of Maine. This day is celebrated every year with the week-long Acadian Festival. Acadian families all over the United States and Canada are invited to attend. In 1994 about four thousand people arrived in Madawaska for the festival. One large family had relatives come from seven Canadian provinces and 25 states!

The festival celebrates Acadian history with a parade, traditional music, dances, and storytelling—all done Acadian style. The festival banquet features Acadian food. A favorite dish is called "pot en pot," which includes seven different kinds of meat. The festival also includes a traditional Acadian Catholic mass. And almost everyone makes a special stop at the Tante Blanche Museum. Tante Blanche was Marguerite Blanche Thibodeau, who lived during the late 1700s. During a hard time in 1797 called the Black Famine, Tante Blanche went from house to house to collect such things as food and clothing. She then shared them with people who were cold, hungry, and sick. The museum houses exhibits that cover the long history of the Acadians.

The Acadians of Madawaska are proud of their culture. Through the annual Acadian Day celebration, they have found a way to introduce their culture to new generations.

Many Acadians plan their family reunions to coincide with the Acadian Festival.

Making the Most of Nature's Gifts

A popular picture of Maine is of someone fishing for lobsters in the cold Atlantic coastal waters. It's easy to see why. Maine is the number one supplier of lobsters in the United States. But Maine's economy goes beyond lobsters.

Maine's agriculture commands a small but significant portion of the state's economy. Maine's soil is rocky and thin, so it isn't surprising that farming makes up only a little more than two percent of the state's economy. Livestock, such as beef cattle and chickens, and livestock products, such as eggs and dairy products, make up almost half of that farm income. Another primary farm product is potatoes. In fact, only two other states, Idaho and Washington, raise more potatoes than Maine. About ninety percent of the Maine potato crop is grown in Aroostook County, which is the largest county east of the Mississippi River.

Field crops, such as hay, oats, and corn, are less important to Maine's farm economy than they are in many other states. Many farmers plant potatoes one

Nearly every community along Maine's coast has its own small fleet of fishing boats.

Eggs account for a large portion of Maine's farm income.

Maine fishers catch ninety percent of the lobster sold throughout the nation.

year and oats the next. That's because potatoes use up much of the soil's nutrients, and oats put nutrients back into the soil. Alternating these two crops helps keep the soil fertile.

Truck farms are common in the southern part of the state. Truck farms grow crops that are driven to local markets. These farms produce mainly sweet corn and peas. In addition, Maine provides 98 percent of the low-bush blueberries in the United States. Maine apples bring in more money, however, because there are more uses for apples. The state also grows strawberries and raspberries.

Lobsters make up the largest part of the fish industry in Maine. Rockport and Rockland are major lobstering centers. More than thirty million pounds of lobster were harvested in Maine in 1993! Maine is second only to Massachusetts in the amount of fish caught every year. In the 1800s so many fish were caught in Maine's waters that the state was called the "New England Silver Mine." Today, Maine's ocean harvest includes perch, herring, pollock, cod, clams, scallops, and shrimp.

Much of Maine's forestland includes what are known as "second-growth" forests. In other words the original trees were cut down long ago, first to make ships and later as part of the state's lumber industry. The trees that now cover about ninety percent of the state were planted by the people of Maine. Most of these forests are owned by corporations that use the wood for various industries.

Manufacturing makes up almost twenty percent of Maine's economy. The major area of Maine manufacturing is paper products made from replanted trees. After the trees are harvested, the paper-making companies grind the wood into a pulp. That pulp is used to make paper products that range from shopping bags to fine stationery. Some companies also use wood pulp to make building products such as particleboard. Other wood products manufactured in Maine include lumber, firewood, and finished wood for construction and fine furniture.

Ninety-eight percent of the nation's wild, low-bush blueberries are grown in Maine.

Maine also manufactures high-tech products, including electronic equipment, especially components, or parts, for computers. Food processing is another important part of Maine's manufacturing industry. Wild blueberries are harvested and quick-frozen in southern Maine. Russet potatoes, grown in the north, are made into French fries. Maine factories pack, can, and otherwise package much of the fish caught along the shore, including sardines, clams, lobsters, and shrimp.

About seventy percent of Maine's economy is taken up by service industries. People in service industries do not make goods to sell. Instead, they do things for people. The largest group of service industries is wholesale and retail trade. Retail trade is selling products to people. Wholesale trade involves selling

Paper is an important manufacturing product in Maine.

Maine is the third largest potato producer in the United States.

L. L. Bean began as a shoe manufacturing company.

products to stores that sell products to people. L. L. Bean, a large mail-order company and clothing retailer, is based in Maine. Other service industries are banking, real estate, government, and community, social, and personal services.

Tourism is another very large part of Maine's economy. The biggest attraction is Maine's coastline, with its 250 miles of bays and inlets. Bar Harbor is the state's most popular tourist area. Maine's wilderness offers spectacular mountain views, forests, and thousands of rivers and lakes. The sports-minded will find plenty of opportunities for skiing, hunting, and fishing as well as for hiking, camping, and canoeing.

Maine is working hard to add new businesses to its economy. For example, the state now has a growing chemicals industry. It is also looking for ways to attract new businesses, especially ones that will provide employment in the less-populated central and northern areas. Maine's goal is for all its citizens to share in and contribute to its economy.

The beauty of Maine's coast in summer is one of the attractions that draws tourists to the state year after year.

Most of these pine trees will someday become Christmas trees.

The Ships and Boats of Bath

The Popham Colony, established in 1607, was the first English settlement in present-day Maine. It lasted less than a year, but during that time the settlers built the first ship in North America. It was a thirty-ton wooden cargo ship called the *Virginia*. Since that time the people of Maine have built ships. Bath was New England's most important shipbuilding town. By 1850 half of the country's merchant vessels were built in Bath.

The traditional skills required to build finely crafted wooden ships have been preserved in Bath at the Maine Maritime Museum. The museum has a school called the Apprenticeshop. Its mission is to "preserve the unique maritime heritage and culture of Maine's seafaring and shipbuilding history."

A course of study at the special Apprenticeshop school takes a year. The classes are small, only 12 students, so that each student can receive individualized instruction from master woodworkers. The main task in the school is to design and construct boats. Students decide what they want to build. In the same class, some students may wish to construct a kayak; others may build a 12-foot-long rowboat; and still others may complete a 30-foot-long sailboat. Some projects can be completed by one student, and others require several. Students use traditional hand tools in making their boats; no electric sanders, saws, or drills are allowed. Students are enthusiastic about their work. As one student said, "Taking time to build something is great. There's a certain joy in having a physical product resulting from your work."

Apprenticeshop students also learn how to restore the original character and beauty to traditional wooden boats and ships. Students are given the opportunity to work on repairing and restoring old boats and ships in the Maritime Museum's collection. Repairing and restoring wooden boats and ships is an uncommon craft. Apprenticeshop students are in demand all over the United States for their special skills.

At the end of the program, students select an independent project. These projects are hands-on opportunities to extend their knowledge of ships. For example, some students are allowed to oversee work at a shipyard. Many projects lead to permanent jobs.

These students have a love for ships. The Apprenticeshop allows them to turn that love into a practical skill.

Apprenticeshop students learn how to repair and restore 150 different kinds of historic boats and ships.

At certain times of the year, tourists in Bath can visit the Apprenticeshop and watch apprentices building and repairing boats by hand.

The Past Is Present

One aspect of Maine's culture is reflected in the people's pride in their heritage. For example, the people of Maine keep the memory of their state's military history alive by restoring its many forts. One very special restored fort is Fort Popham, built in 1861 at the time of the Civil War. Fort Popham is near the site of the original Popham Colony, Maine's first permanent European colony, established in 1607. Some of the other forts, such as Fort Knox, feature re-creations of the way people lived during those times.

Maine's shipbuilding history holds a place of honor in Maine's culture. The Maine Maritime Museum in Bath has collections of marine paintings, ship models, and photographs. The museum also features demonstrations of traditional wooden boat-building techniques. Sailing is still an essential part of Maine's culture. Every July Boothbay Harbor presents its Windjammer Festival. The festival features a gathering of windjammer sailing ships, a parade of antique ships, as well as fireworks over the bay.

This painting by Andrew Wyeth is called "Northern Point, 1950." Wyeth was enchanted by the stark beauty of Maine's landscapes.

This is one of 16 stone bridges in Acadia National Park. Each bridge has been individually designed for its surroundings.

No festival in Maine would be complete without a group of musicians gathered together to entertain visitors.

Maine's history of logging is remembered at the Dead River Historical Society Museum in Stratton. The museum features artifacts from early loggers and displays nineteenth-century town life, including a typical schoolhouse. In Bangor visitors can tour the home of Isaac Farrar, who made a fortune in the lumber business. Bangor was the most important lumber-exporting community in the world in the 1850s, and Farrar was one of the reasons why. His carefully restored mansion features marble fireplaces, carved woodwork, and stained-glass windows.

American writers have found Maine to be a perfect place to work. In the nineteenth century, Henry Wadsworth Longfellow produced his famous poem about Acadia, called *Evangeline*. Another Maine author, Sarah Orne Jewett, was one of the first recognized women authors in America. Many critics believe her best novel is *The Country of the Pointed Firs*, about life in a small town along the coast of Maine. Edna St. Vincent Millay, who was born in Rockland, received the Pulitzer Prize in 1923 for *The Harp-Weaver and Other Poems*. Today, the most famous Maine writer is Stephen King. His books of horror and fantasy have also been turned into successful movies.

The people of Maine have always had a deep respect for their natural environment. Baxter State Park, in the center of the state, includes Mount Katahdin, Maine's mile-high mountain, plus many lakes, rivers, and acres of untouched forests. The land of this park, about two hundred thousand acres, was owned by former governor Percival P. Baxter. He gave the land to the state "to be forever left in its natural state." There are many other natural areas in Maine that are popular with tourists. One of these is the Appalachian Trail, which was blazed by Native Americans and followed by settlers. At Snow Falls Gorge, people can still dig for gemstones such as tourmaline, garnet, and quartz. Many of Maine's ski resorts, such as Sugarloaf, are internationally known.

People in Maine celebrate their fishing tradition at the Lobster Festival in Rockland and at the World's Fastest Lobsterboat Race in Jonesboro. The summer is a time when residents take to the water, whether they raft down wild rivers in the interior of the state, kayak in the bays, or sail across ocean waters.

What is dearest to the people of Maine is the natural environment. Logging and fishing provide people in Maine with livelihoods. Outdoor activities, such as hiking and skiing, are an important part of leisure time. In this way, the people of Maine are linked to the land and the sea.

Henry Wadsworth Longfellow enjoyed great popularity in Europe as well as in the United States. His poems have been translated into many languages.

Harriet Beecher Stowe was living in Brunswick when she wrote her novel *Uncle Tom's Cabin* in 1852, not long before the Civil War. This antislavery novel helped turn public opinion in the North against slavery.

Maine Music Produces a Classic

In 1969 Paul Vermel, then the conductor of the Portland Symphony Orchestra, had an idea. He wanted to hire a group of four world-class professional musicians to play in the orchestra. In return for higher salaries, the four musicians also agreed to perform special concerts in Maine schools. They later began giving concerts in other cities. That was the beginning of the Portland String Quartet. Today, the PSQ, as it is often known, is recognized as one of the greatest string quartets in the world.

A string quartet is a group of four musicians playing string instruments. Quartet compositions usually require two violins, a viola, and a cello. Violinists Stephen Kecskemethy and Ronald Lantz, violist Julia Adams, and cellist Paul Ross are the current members of the PSQ. String quartets usually play a type of classical music called chamber music, which first became popular in Europe in the 1700s. Chamber music was performed by small groups of musicians in private homes, usually for a gathering of

The members of the Portland String Quartet explain the basics of music to a young group of students.

40

In 1993 the Portland String Quartet celebrated its 25th anniversary.

friends. Today, chamber music is still played for small gatherings, but string quartets also perform concerts in large halls.

Since 1979 the PSQ has given concerts in the finest concert halls in the United States, such as Carnegie Hall in New York City. The group has performed all over Europe, South America, Japan, and Russia. Arabesque and Northeastern records have signed PSQ to recording contracts. In 1984 PSQ's recording of Ernest Bloch's string quartets was rated the best chamber music record in the country. In 1985 the quartet was nominated for a

Grammy. The PSQ has become so well known that new composers write music just for the group. Even with this busy schedule, the PSQ still plays concerts for schools all over Maine. The musicians also teach classes at Colby College, which awarded them honorary doctorate degrees in 1986.

The members of the PSQ say that they have the best of all possible worlds. They travel all over the world and play for huge audiences in large cities. They return to live in a state with natural beauty, where the pace of life is calm. For the Portland String Quartet, Maine is the best place to call home.

Choosing a Future

Maine faces many challenges as it looks toward the future. In the last ten years, the state's population has grown by ten percent. Most of that growth has occurred in a relatively small region along the coast. Increased population means more homes are clustered along the shore. It also means an increase in the demand for social services, such as schools, hospitals, and police and fire departments. More people mean more stores, malls, and roads.

The people of Maine aren't sure how this growth will affect the beauty of their state. State and local governments have begun to look into ways to control the amount of development that does occur. For instance, a town can use a regulation called zoning to control the kinds of buildings that are built in a particular area. Zoning will allow a strip mall to be built in a business zone but not in a neighborhood zone. Maine citizens don't want to put an end to growth; they just want to be careful about how they grow.

Portland has many strengths which will help to carry it into the future. It is a center for transportation, commercial fishing, shipbuilding, and finance.

Retail stores, such as L. L. Bean in Freeport, are subject to local zoning laws.

On the other hand, in the central and northern parts of Maine, there has been very little growth. Many lumber companies in those regions now use automated equipment instead of human workers. As a result, unemployment is a serious problem. In this part of the state, Maine citizens encourage development. They are also careful to protect the rugged beauty of the region.

Recently many skills that were important to the early development of the state have again become a source of income and employment in Maine. These skills include shipbuilding, weaving, and pottery. These skills are also very useful in restoring historic buildings and neighborhoods. The state actively supports the growth of these small businesses.

The people of Maine have always been independent. They also consider their options carefully before they act. Those qualities will guide Maine citizens in the future, as they work to meet new challenges that may arise.

Important Historical Events

1000	Vikings explore the coast of present-day Maine.
1498	John Cabot probably explores the northern Atlantic coast.
1524	Giovanni da Verrazano explores the coast of present-day Maine.
1525	Estéban Gomez explores the coast and names several bays.
1598	Sir Humphrey Gilbert sends a ship to claim the territory of Maine for England.
1603	King Henry IV of France gives Acadia to Pierre du Gast, Sieur de Monts.
1604	Du Gast establishes a colony on Dochet's Island. Samuel de Champlain explores Maine.
1605	Du Gast moves his colony to present-day Nova Scotia.
1607	The Popham Colony is established.
1613	A French Catholic mission is built on Mount Desert Island.
1622	England grants Sir Ferdinando Gorges and John Mason much of the land of Maine and New Hampshire.
1629	The Gorges-Mason grant is divided in two, and Gorges is given the upper half.
1641	Gorgeana—today called York—becomes the region's first chartered English city.
1652	Massachusetts Bay Colony takes over the governing of the province of Maine.
1763	The Treaty of Paris ending the French and Indian War is signed.
1774	Maine citizens burn a supply of British tea at York.
1775	Americans and British fight the first naval battle of the Revolutionary War off the coast of Maine.
1783	Maine's eastern boundary is fixed at the St. Croix River.
1820	Maine becomes the twenty-third state.
1832	Augusta becomes the state capital.
1842	The signing of the Webster-Ashburton Treaty ends disputes over the Maine-Canada border.
1851	Maine makes it illegal to manufacture or sell alcoholic beverages in the state.
1880	The Bath Iron Works opens.
1940	Margaret Chase Smith begins 33 years of public service.
1955	Maine establishes a Department of Economic Development to draw new businesses to the state.
1965	Gold deposits are found near Pembroke.
1969	Maine passes a law taxing both personal and corporate incomes.
1976	Voters approve a forty-thousand-acre wilderness preserve on Bigelow Mountain in Somerset County.
1980	The Passamaquoddy and the Penobscot win their lawsuit against the federal government.
1988	Maine and nine other states sue the Environmental Protection Agency.
1994	Maine refuses to follow clean-air regulations on auto emissions, claiming that its air problems are caused by industries in states to the west.

The state flag shows the state seal on a blue background. On the seal, a farmer and a seaman represent the state's main industries. A pine tree symbolizes the state's vast forestland. The moose stands for Maine's wilderness. Above the seal is the state motto.

Maine Almanac

Nickname. The Pine Tree State

Capital. Augusta

State Bird. Chickadee

State Flower. White pine cone and tassel

State Tree. White pine

State Motto. *Dirigo* (I lead)

State Song. "State of Maine Song"

State Abbreviations. Me. (traditional); ME (postal)

Statehood. March 15, 1820, the 23rd state

Government. Congress: U.S. senators, 2; U.S. representatives, 2. State Legislature: senators, 35; representatives, 151. Counties: 16

Area. 33,128 sq mi (85,801 sq km), 39th in size among the states

Greatest Distances. north/south, 303 mi (488 km); east/west, 202 mi (325 km). Shoreline: 228 mi (367 km)

Elevation. Highest: Mount Katahdin, 5,268 ft (1,606 m). Lowest: sea level, along the Atlantic Ocean

Population. 1990 Census: 1,233,223 (10% increase over 1980), 38th among the states. Density: 37 persons per sq mi (14 persons per sq km). Distribution: 55% rural, 45% urban. 1980 Census: 1,125,030

Economy. *Agriculture*: eggs, milk, beef cattle, hogs, sheep, lambs, turkeys, potatoes, oats, beans, peas, sugar beets. *Fishing*: lobsters, clams, perch, scallops, herring, shrimp. *Manufacturing*: paper and wood products, textiles, leather, processed foods, electric and electronic equipment, automotive equipment, shipbuilding. *Mining*: sand and gravel, granite, crushed stone, limestone, clay, copper, zinc, gemstones

State Seal

State Flower: White pine cone and tassel

State Bird: Chickadee

Annual Events

★ Downeast Tennis Classic in Portland (May)

★ Clam Festival in Yarmouth (July)

★ Maine Broiler Festival in Belfast (July)

★ Windjammer Days, at Boothbay Harbor (July)

★ Blueberry Festival in Union (August)

★ Maine Seafoods Festival in Rockland (August)

★ State Fair in Lewiston (September)

Places to Visit

★ Acadia National Park in south-eastern Maine

★ Black Mansion in Ellsworth

★ Burnham Tavern in Machias

★ Fort Western in Augusta

★ Old Gaol Museum in York

★ Penobscot Marine Museum in Searsport

★ Portland Head Light, near Portland

★ Tate House in Portland

★ Wadsworth-Longfellow House in Portland

★ White Mountain National Forest in southwestern Maine

47